four-legged girl

Books by Diane Seuss

It Blows You Hollow
Wolf Lake, White Gown Blown Open
Four-Legged Girl
Still Life with Two Dead Peacocks and a Girl
frank: sonnets
Modern Poetry

four-legged girl

poems

DIANE SEUSS

Graywolf Press

This publication is made possible, in part, by the voters of Minnesota through a Minnesota State Arts Board Operating Support grant, thanks to a legislative appropriation from the arts and cultural heritage fund, and through grants from the National Endowment for the Arts and the Wells Fargo Foundation Minnesota. Significant support has also been provided by Target, the McKnight Foundation, Amazon.com, and other generous contributions from foundations, corporations, and individuals. To these organizations and individuals we offer our heartfelt thanks.

Published by Graywolf Press
212 Third Avenue North, Suite 485
Minneapolis, Minnesota 55401

www.graywolfpress.org

Published in the United States of America

ISBN 978-1-55597-722-1

6 8 10 12 11 9 7 5

Library of Congress Control Number: 2015939976

Cover design: Jeenee Lee Design

Cover photo: Charles Eisenman, *Myrtle Corbin,* 1882

For my people:
the living and the dead

Contents

iv. free beer

v. a period's period

see the sensational
two-headed woman
one face turned outward
one face
swiveling slowly in

Lucille Clifton, "in this garden"

four-legged girl

i. blossomhouse

Jump rope song

Beautiful blankness, I saw you once
in a bucket of glue, on the flank of a horse with glass eyes,

in a gown and the girl's ankles were shaking,

in Dream Whip, in hawk shit, in comfrey, cress,
campion, potato vine, pokeweed, lopseed, the dodder,

the clover and the honeysuckle flower, white as boiled bone.

White as boiled bone until it yellows,
like the poof of hair on nursing-home women, Bunco dice,

scrimshaw of the HMS *Agamemnon* on a sperm-whale tooth,

hind quarters of a white-tailed deer, hind end
of a hare, of a Welsh cow who's born like milk and dies like butter.

Born like milk and dies like butter, like batter after you add the eggs,

those orbs with a beating heart inside, yellow foam
on the lake by the bowling alley, blank pins gone gold,

and the trophy mother won, and her rayon sweater soaked in beer.

Her rayon sweater soaked in beer, her ivory hand mirror
turning toward amber, glass of the hurricane lamp and the monocle,

the paper holding the poem about the monocle, even the floor, gold.

Even the floorboards. Rag rug. Lamb nightlight. Waning
moonlight on hospital sheets on the line, and the christening gown

brushed with pollen, cut into costumes for canaries.

Costumes for canaries, for lovebirds, aprons for dolls, all
lined up under the mock orange tree, and where is the girl serving

buttermilk in thimbles, is the girl in the blossomhouse gone?

As a child I ate and mourned

Now I will not eat. I will not mourn.

Bowls of glistening peaches.

Bowls of them, I tell you.
Golden, with a menstrual stain where the pit was pulled away.

On one of my daily strolls into the next-door cemetery
I encountered the hog snake, which even then was put on earth
to represent the antithesis of the working stiff.

The funeral director set a house trailer
on the cemetery edge to serve as a chapel
for grievers. It was cold in there, even in summer,
the paneling warped.

A cheap box of tissues on the card table.
I slid one out and balled it up, stuck it in my mouth.
Those were paper-eating days.

The gravedigger, his shovel carried over his shoulder like a musket.

I was pure of soul. I was.
Chosen to play the angel in every drama about God.
I had things in the right order:
i.e. the body is but a playhouse for the soul, all that.

It seems, back then, there was a mythic teapot

A napkin holder shaped like a garden gate with painted
trumpet vines. The old couple whose goodness was unassailable.
They slapped their knees when they laughed at our antics,
which were really not that funny. Chewing graham crackers
into the shapes of guns. The old couple, Mr. and Mrs. Riddle.

Their drab mouths, their teeth in a jar, their dishes and glassware
the color of the amber that traps mosquitos. Their house edged
in yellow gladiolas I called flower pokers. My father's tumors
bloomed like thought balloons in cartoons but inside them was
only a sigh. My mother set her hair on fire leaning over a lit

cake and it seems her hair was on fire for many days. Or was that
the lady with the red bouffant whose big thighs shook when she
walked up the sidewalk toward the place called Beauty, where she
got her hair piled and pinned. The mice in our house were tame,
willingly incorporating themselves into our games. Tail hanging out

of the dollhouse window. A wasp hid in my underpants and stung
my biscuit. My mother called it my biscuit. My father said that's
the way of wasps or he thought it and I read it in the big white
moonflower that hung above him, attached by a green umbilical
cord. He'd walk to work every day, thin suit, boot-polish hair.

Hope was a vinegar-colored halo that formed around our heads.
It came and went, like fighting and fireflies. From the schoolyard
I could see my mother holding a basket of wet laundry
with clothespins in her mouth. It was strange to watch my own
dresses and blouses swaying on the line. As if I'd been skinned alive.

The potato sack filled with toys was beautiful

though the toys were evil. A wooden, jointed snake.
Not a cowboy gun but a black revolver. A jack-in-the-box
that played a warped Chopin nocturne, and you don't

want to know who leaped out of the box. There were
features to be pressed into a potato to make a face
but the essential ones were missing. What was left?

A pipe. A monocle. A pair of juicy female lips. No wonder
the old woman kept the sack in the attic where the flying
squirrels hung from the rafters. But when I visited,

which was often, she'd creep down the narrow stairway —
all the woodwork in the house was a slick, lacquered
walnut— and deliver the sack into my open arms.

Out of those few objects I built my dubious lexicon.
There was a hand mirror, and a naked baby doll.
And a pink-nippled bottle for the child filled with what

had long ago been a milky liquid but was now the color
of absinthe, once known as "la fée verte," the Green Fairy.

People, the ghosts down in North-of-the-South aren't see-through

They don't wear nightgowns or whisper or sing
or want hazy things from the ones of us who are living.
They have skin, bones, people. They're short in stature
and they don't walk through walls. They come in our houses

by kicking down doors, wearing porkpie hats and smoking
those My Father cigars. Yellow sweat stains
on their sleeveless undershirts, my people. I'm sure
there are other kinds of ghosts other places,

sad angels wearing bloomers and fanning their wings,
but here their faces are made of gristle and their eyes
are red from too much Thunderbird. They want to steal
our valuables, mess shit up, drop a match and burn

down the house. I don't know any other way to say it,
people. They walk right into our kitchens without being invited,
tracking mud, lifting the fish by the tail out of the fryer
and stuffing it in a cloth sack the color of a potato

just pulled out of the ground, and if there was a potato
pulled fresh out of the ground they'd take that too.
Their pee sizzles when it hits the floor. They don't hear
prayers or heed four-leaf clovers. We have to give

our bodies to the task. I mean we push back, people.
Harder than day labor. Harder than shoving a bull
out of the cow paddock. Two bulls. We have to say
leave my goddamned house. Go, motherfucker.

My fucking house. Shouting while pushing, like breach birth,
or twins. They slap on that corpse-smelling aftershave
and come calling, holding a bouquet of weeds. They want
our whiskey, our gravy, our honey, our combs, our bees.

An occasion is a rare occasion

Rare as a bloodbath in a barn. In our county,
not one bloodbath in a barn, but a redbird
in a birdbath is ho-hum. A field is ho-hum.
A horizon is just a girl yawning at the edge

of a field holding a long, curved stick.
She remembers reading ho-hum in a book
and it was odd to her though not odd
enough to be an occasion. Rhubarb leaves

curling up out of the dirt in the spring
are not an occasion. Things that happen
on their own without help are ho-hum
like popping out a baby but a baby shower

is an occasion, a small occasion but it counts.
There are cupcakes to be frosted blue
and balloons to blow up with the breath
of our own bodies though now

there are helium tanks. Have you sucked in
enough? Did your voice sound high
and strange? That is a miniature occasion,
but then your voice goes back to its usual

ragged self so in the end sucking helium
is a temporary occasion. All occasions
are temporary in our county. A silo in a field
is ho-hum but if it burns it is a temporary

occasion. So many things burn that fires
are in danger of becoming ho-hum.
Only the strange fires count.
The supermarket fire with its exploding

jars of pickles, the outdoor movie-screen fire.
The firehouse fire. In our county
clouds are bags heavy with empties
gathered from parking lots of strip malls

and shut-down pattern factories.
Soon there will be enough to cash in.
Soon the sky will rain quarters.
Enough for bread and bologna

and squares of American cheese
and cereal shaped like stars. The milk
in the bowl will go pink with the pinkness
of the stars. That will be an occasion.

Hub

I. My first rainshade was sun-blasted,

with room enough for boys. Then came one covered in umber-colored horses,
which galloped, when I had the wherewithal to spin the crook handle, like figures

in a zoetrope. The kids on 17th St. called themselves the Dismantlers, stripping
away the canopy from the ribs and stretchers and hollowing out the wooden

shafts, filling them with gumballs and wild onions. My father was cynical
about the whole enterprise. He'd walk in the rain like his tumors were made

of sugar. It's not like my mother donated her skirts and dresses after he died.
They just disappeared, absorbed into the wall at the back of her closet.

She rescinded anything shelter-shaped, including the parasol flowers. The wind
was our theatre, dramatically turning all bells inside-out: school bell, church bell,

dinner bell. We became known as the town whose clappers were stolen by a series
of gusts from the west. The only thing that tolled was the toll road. When Wanda

gave up taxidermy and became a Jehovah's Witness, some of us absconded with her
impressive collection of stuffed predatory birds, wings extended in mid-flight.

I impaled mine, a barn owl with blue glass eyes, on a long copper tube I found
at the shut-down pattern factory. I brandished my owl like a papal umbraculum

whose purpose had nothing to do with weather, not shade but shadow. A mayoral
candidate ran on a platform of installing a velarium over the town, a sort of awning,

the corners tied to city limit signs, like the retractable one at the Roman Coliseum.
He was defeated in a landslide. The minister's final sermon had a catchy title:

There Is No Protection. Not Really. Even my mother nodded at that one,
the smoke from her Viceroy entangled in her unwrangled curls.

II. Was there ever a time that I bothered to stay dry?

In my previous incarnation
I didn't mind the flagellum
made of peacock feathers,
held over my head during

cavalcades. You see, I had
yet to be humbled. In New
York, buoyed by the blowsy
vapors of young love,

I carried a lacquered paper one
on a balsa handle, spring
green painted
with white violets, but only

to cut a romantic figure,
a small-breasted lusted-after
girl flouncing off
to the secretarial pool.

Wetness was a way of life,
upping the saturation
of my little white blouses
and beading my eyelashes

with prisms. Translucency
served my purposes,
which were transparent
as glass shoes. "Who's

the queen now?" He said it
in a lilting manner, the man
wearing bright yellow rain gear.
I hate foreshadowing.

III. The umbrella was the hub,

and the hub of the umbrella was the pole around which the cleats and skeleton ribs spun. From the hub arose many begettings. The peony was begotten, the woody stem echoing the umbrella pole, topped by the beguiling trivialities of petals, and the peony begat the Heartland Peony Society, which begat culture. Culture begat the faux peony, the petals sometimes made of silk, the stem, a hub of cold wire wrapped in green tape, which begat capitalism, which in turn begat tilt-o-whirls, tennis skirts and fireworks, all things that spin and flare for no reason other than the fact that spinning and flaring greases the machine, which begat the idea for a solar system—bodies circling the hubs of other bodies—which begat weather, and Christmas, which begat shopping, and denial—thus, our decision to believe that the ants crawling over the unbloomed heads of peonies were somehow rehabilitative. The lie begat love begat sex begat rabbits that lurked beneath the protective leaves of wild mandrake during rainstorms which begat the maypole, a hub with ribbons, and girls. Ma and Pa called things by their real names. *Peony,* they said, the word that begat us. We begat the euphemism. *God,* we said, looking at the umbrella impaled dead center in the lamb barn.

IV. What was intriguing was not what the man took with him;

it was the stuff he left behind.
He took the butterflies

but left the moths. He took
Krishna but left Shiva.

He left the cumbersome
fishing boat and sinkers

and musky lures but took
the poles and spinner reels.

He left the kid but took the toys.
The man rented a storage locker

and filled it with everything
he'd brought with him

from the old life, but after two
months he stopped remembering

to pay the rental fee. Everything
was confiscated and put up

for auction, the bleach bottle
filled with marbles, the Sorry

game, the thousand-piece puzzle
of the Parthenon, the big statue

of the thundercloud-colored
god of love. He left behind,

in the corner of the house's
entryway, a long black umbrella

with a carved lion's head handle,
but took with him the invaluable

praxinoscope, its circle of mirrors
and whirling cylinder

of hand-painted pictures
of a woman walking in the rain.

Spirea's covered in those clotted blooms

as a newborn's coated by vernix. Irises rise up on meaty stems,
buds still wrapped in something like rolling papers,
purple pressing through, the color of entrails.

You see, I've noticed. See, I've seen. I have more eyes than a potato
bug has legs. More fears than eyes, or tears.

At night I walk beneath the apple tree, the plum, the weeping cherry.
Their cloak of blossoms is a heavy load,
as is a head of waist-length hair and the wedding dress of that princess,

so slight in flesh but draped in velvet hyacinths, and pearls like sinkers,
and rhinestones like salt tears frozen in the maiden's eyes

in "The Wreck of the Hesperus." I loved that girl, lashed to the mast of her father's ship,
her hair rising and falling like seaweed on the billows.
I wanted beauty like that, beauty that turned my dying eyes to cold, heavy jewels,

and love like that, so stupid and blind it would preserve me by killing me.
But now. Here, mid-May, past prime,

the tulips brown and splay like washed-up things,
and the glory girls have stepped out of their gowns, set down their racks,
unlatched their trains. Beauty was a burden after all, wasn't it?

And love. I remember it like some wet, leggy foal
I had to hold in my arms for nights on end to keep it warm.

Love was an unmothered thing, for the mother of love was heartless.
I held on, as branches hold shivering sparrows in their arms,
and a hundred little hollow nests like crowns of thorns.

Maybe the fishmonger, who hands over the dead

so tenderly or maybe the one rolling sushi wearing
a hairnet and a half-smile or maybe no one, for I have held

hands with a stone, I have held hands with an orphaned
poplar tree whose leaves chattered like the milk teeth of a kid

left for dead in a woven basket. I have held the freckled,
sun-burnished face of the lily and stroked her with my palm,

my fingerprints overwhelmed by her rusty pollen. Maybe
her, maybe the aproned fishmonger, who has held hands

with a boning knife and brushed away crushed ice
from the cloudy eye and rid the pinkish flesh of pin bones,

or no one, for when I was a girl I held my father's cold
hand and he wore something like an apron, a cotton gown

fastened with bows at the back, a gown covered in blue
stars, and his black eyelashes splayed out like the open arms

of starfish, and oh he was sad, there was salt in his cloudy
eye, and something swam up into my throat and spawned

and flapped its great tail, so perhaps I'm adrift in a skiff
spiraling the hub of that tender sea, or maybe

the fishmonger, maybe the mute cashier, or no one,
or never, or the ancient bagger tattooed with an anchor.

White violet, not so much an image

of tenderness as an image of a memory of tenderness. I am ashamed

to look at it this closely but can't stop fingering

its five sticky petals, nebulous as water on the brink

of becoming steam. Thin as a soul lingering for three days

threatening to reignite into flesh, or a ghost

climbing the body's bone ladder in order to abdicate

the body's terms.

This flower might as well be a girl named Violet, with dew on her upper lip,

who elopes through her bedroom window, leaving only

her thin, yellow-white chemise behind. Its petals are that fragile.

They lack commitment to the material world, their molecules ascending,

any minute now, evaporative, like a pretty infant bound

and determined to fly back into the hands of nothingness,

or a shepherd dispassionate about the lambs, always looking off

into the lavender beyond.

The only way to know tenderness is to dismantle it.

That's the essential problem, how we must get out the jeweler's loupe

and start dissecting, prying open the mauve sac

at the base of the flower

like a fox in the henhouse, looking for green ovaries spilling over with eggs,

or Hawthorne's Aylmer, prying away at Georgiana's birthmark.

I bring the torn flower to my mouth to confirm

the myth of its honey, only to find it tastes gamey, green, like a hand

that's held too long to copper coins. This close, its scent is not sweet

but sour—I crush it to awaken its perfumes—acidic, unripe,

puerile, stinging, tined.

I remember a poet reading translations of Paul Valéry when I was

young. I wore a white, gauzy dress with laces at the bodice,

and the poet stood in a pool of heroic white-gold light

with his shirt half-unbuttoned, his silver hair curling over his ears.

"Perfume is what the flowers throw away," he read, quoting Valéry.

Later he tried to pry me open, but I ran home barefoot through the rain

under a foggy membrane of moon—that ventricular patch

sewed between the chambers of night and day,

that wispy peephole in the screen between supplicant and priest

in the confessional booth, that rice-paper privacy screen

painted with a profusion of white violets in the black bordello.

ii. blowtorch the hinges

I once fought the idea of the body as artifact,

my hair hanging long, romancing my waist. Down by the creek with my baby,
marsh marigolds slick as melted butter. His hair sticking up in small flames
like the choir-boy candles we dragged out of the mausoleum each December,

their wax mouths holding a pure note for decades. I was nebulous as an amoeba
or a nebula, hot water bottle with a flimsy skin, my clothes flowed, my eyes

changed color in the fall, my horse was made of rainwater. The key
to the transformation was eyeliner, eyeliner and a series of deaths. I began
to outline my eyes in kohl designed for the stage. Gold wristbands from

Woolworth's downtown and long, body-hugging shifts I designed and sewed
in Home Ec class, uneven seams, metallic thread. I cut bangs with pinking shears

and hardened my bob with Dippity-Do, my eyelashes fixed into black points
like the minute hand on my dead father's watch. I embarked on an affair
with my English teacher, a hairy man with a barrel chest who brought a bottle

of Cuervo in his briefcase to our house when my mother was at the gambling
boat. You think you're immortal, he said, but you're not. I'd learned how

to hold my face still, my whole body still, even when I waxed the big slide
at Kelly's Sportsland, two pieces of waxed paper under a burlap sack during
the lunar eclipse. I wore a lip gloss that made my mouth look like glass and rode

the frisky horse of time, mane braided with stars, down the serpentine humps
of the slide. A stone horse, but I was flying.

Long, long ago I used to smoke in bed

I lived in the basement of an old Victorian,
in a converted coal room with a single bed
built into the wall. I owned nothing, nothing,
and I liked it that way. Well, not absolutely
nothing. I'd picked up a chair somewhere
along the way. Red velour, an over-soft
swaybacked thing with a matching ottoman.
Along the way, also, a cardboard box
full of tangled costume jewelry. Fake topaz,
tourmaline, zircon the color of a white rabbit's
eyes. A choker strung with clanking mock emeralds.
I was beautiful, yes I was. Not so much beautiful
to the world. I was too short and round for that,
my ankles too thick, like a peasant's. Working-class
teeth. Working-class hand-me-down bras.
But beautiful to myself, yes, yes, and to some,
striking enough to be desired. I hennaed my hair
the color of that wicked chair. My jewels shone.
What else is there to say? Did I work? When I read,
did I read closely? I know I transcribed tapes
for a local author. Tapes of his interviews
with a serial killer, conducted at the state penitentiary
in Jackson. For hours at a time, that killer whispered
in my ear, droning on about his gruesome misdeeds
like a mosquito or a husband. I forgot to say
I'd discovered Rimbaud by then. His jaundiced
point of view had ruined me. Every flower, every tree,
every stone was inked purple by his stinking, ornate
arrogance. I sat in the chair and smoked. The chair
swallowed me, and I smoked. I lay flat on my back
in that cold bed and smoked. Sometimes long-haired
girls brought their boyfriends to visit and we shared
that old Michigan combo, beer with a chaser
of peppermint schnapps. It offers a certain kind
of drunkenness that verges on hallucination,

forlorn and mentholated. I wanted nothing
to do with liqueurs, amaretto washing sentimental
over my blue veins, or some warm-hearted poet's
warm-hearted poems. I didn't even know
there was such a thing as a warm-hearted poem.
I only knew that bitchy boy's poems, Arthur Rimbaud.
It wasn't the drunk boys who wanted me.
It was the girls. It wasn't my body they were drawn to,
but my life, the weird underworld I had going for me,
the basement's hissing pipes and mute, mutant
crickets, the bed in the wall, the red throne
attended to by rats and flying squirrels. The shimmer
of the serial killer's stories, which entered
through my ear and exited, at times, from my lips.
The boyfriends got mad, not at their girls but at me,
for I'd glutted the carburetor of the engine that kept
the world spinning in their direction. I always ended up
kicking them both out, the girl clawing at the tattered
edge of the black slip I wore for clothes, trying to force
her way back into my orbit. Did I say that house
was topped by a glass cupola? And a ghost.
Some lovelorn rich girl pressing her face to the glass
waiting for the return of her fiancée, a lout, an opera
singer, a tenor. You know he was a tenor. I could hear
her up there, pacing the widow's walk in her red velvet
slippers. I'd lay there smoking menthols. Salems,
a brand born the same year I was, named after
that town out east where jackasses burned witches.
My bed was cold back then, and I was cold in it.

I can't stop thinking of that New York skirt, turquoise sequins glued onto sea-colored cotton

I bought it on E. 7th St. in a shop that was only open for one day. Kerouac used to live in that building, but he was dead by then. No zippers or buttons, just strips of fabric to tie on either side of the waist. If I had been one to twirl . . . but I wasn't one to twirl. Still, the skirt worked like honey to flies. Many secret boyfriends, men who'd match their gait to mine and ask for my phone number. I craved tenderness, it's that simple. When the cat was let out of the bag, my real boyfriend would beat them up, bloody their noses. The real boyfriend was clean for ten years, then OD'd out of the blue. Out of the blue of that skirt, some would say. He's buried in a whaling cemetery, looking out to sea. Don't ask me why. I was uninvited from that graveside service. Now I have a limp and the skirt is gone. Why do I have a limp? It involved a pair of little red shoes, a half-size too large. Soles like glass.

It wasn't a dream, I knew William Burroughs

but not well. I was barely more than a girl, and he did not care
for girls. I never got an invitation to his place, a converted urinal

on the Bowery, even after he read my novel *Tongue Talent,* written
under the pseudonym Harry Stick—I was desperate for money

by then—my boyfriend was stealing me blind to feed his habit.
Burroughs would have peed on my poetry, but he loved my porn,

deemed it brilliant, and so I became a minor star for a few days
among the members of his entourage. All I remember of that book

was that it earned me $1,500 and its heroine was Kandy Kakes,
who did it with snakes and horses. Victor, a co-worker at my real job

where I was a secretary and he was the Xerox boy, leaned over
my shoulder as I typed—*Have her do it with a horse,* he said. *Have her*

do it with a snake. He moonlighted as a minor drag queen and seemed
to know something about sex. What did I know? Only that it got me

pregnant, and that those few weeks before I took the walk of shame
into the Margaret Sanger Center, I craved tuna fish sandwiches.

Still, by the time she's sixteen, every girl knows how to think dirty
and how to waitress or type fast enough to get a job slinging hash,

or words. I served drinks for a while at a reggae club, the Negril,
but it didn't take long for all of my Midwestern seams to show.

Then I sold rubber clothes in a fetish shop, but couldn't work the cash
register. I was a nanny, but quit when the kids got lice. I landed

in the secretary's chair with a sigh of relief. That I could do—sitting,
smoking, typing memos for condescending assholes and writing romances

and porn on the side, now and then a poem. The money I made paid
for the rent-controlled apartment roiling with cockroaches on E. 7th St.

and disappeared into my boyfriend's arm. A soup bone, now and then,
wrapped in brown paper from the butcher on 2nd Ave. My boyfriend

told me, years later, in our last phone conversation before he overdosed,
that Burroughs taught him well, jammed that first needle

in his forearm and sat watchfully nearby, hunched over, wearing a face
like a buzzard. It wasn't a dream, I was there when they filmed a scene

from *Naked Lunch* for a documentary on Burroughs, my boyfriend
on camera, his best friend, Howard, the director, who would later die

of AIDS, on whose lips my boyfriend would plant a last kiss. Burroughs
played a doctor, covered in fake blood, with Jackie Curtis as his nurse, all

done up in a Marilyn Monroe wig. I stood on the sidelines wearing a vintage
muskrat coat—those were fur-wearing days. *You're delicious,* Jackie said to me.

I think she thought I was in drag too, my eyeliner curlicuing onto my temple,
my long hair like a spillage of blue ink, and I was, playing girlfriend, playing

secretary, sexpot, writer. Beneath it all I was a farm girl watching locusts devour
the crops, wondering what all the fuss was about. At the office they called me

White Girl, another name for dumbass, innocent, a word they wouldn't have
resorted to, but if they did it would have tasted bitter in their mouths. There is

no redemption in having outlived them all, but having outlived Burroughs, that
makes me smile a bit on the inside, though you'd never know it to look at me.

Warhol's *Shadows*

I can place us in space, the Heiner Friedrich gallery,
393 West Broadway, an exhibit of Andy Warhol's *Shadows*.
I can place us in time, 1979, winter, muddy slush
seeping through the cracks in my shoes. Only the rich
wore heels then, beauty less prescribed, blousier, the light
less filtered then, even in New York, where I blew soot from my nose,
and the homeless, not yet rounded-up, frozen blue on park benches,
or clustered in trinities or quartets, wreathing burn barrels,
smoke helixing into the sky which was often blue,
very often blue, cloudless, a cold January.

A strange, unfiltered innocence, as if the nerves of light
had been stripped, or had never been armored, and I was unarmed,
soft, stupid, not yet muffled by useless wisdom and silly ambitions
which are stand-ins for exhilaration and what is called love, sweet
until it was bitter, and when it was bitter I spat it out
onto the street, which glittered, in winter, with road salt,
fish scales, sequins and spare change.

We didn't intend to go to Warhol's show, intended nothing
in those days, unintended our way into desire,
pregnancy, addiction, Hep C, art, oceans, punk, and later, death,
but then, in the present tense, we wandered
into Warhol's Shadows. The image circled us, caped,
canvases skirting the room like the bell of a jellyfish,
iterative, alliterative, a tolling black echo
against the mopped-on yellow and aubergine, chartreuse and indigo.

I wasn't used to color saturation in those days, our clothes, black,
our hair, our beans, our three rooms on E. 7th nearly windowless,
the roaches, brown, their egg purses dark, the newborns,
translucent amber. Color something we'd have to earn,
like jewels or heaven, and Warhol had applied it, with diamond dust,
extravagantly. There was beauty in it, or a willingness to be beautiful,
expressiveness, gesture, no irony, not the emptiness he was known for,

or the currency, the numbness. The shadows were numinous,
furred, like night is furred, and dreams, the kind we'd wake from
drooling and shouting as if we were children.

Warhol was there, a column of chalk at dead center of the gallery,
signing copies of *Interview.* I think I told him his art was pretty,
which didn't merit even an eye roll or a glance, for I was no one,
a punk in a sea of punks, hooked to a doomed junkie.
I had no identity that Warhol could recognize—identity—
that pale, flat, cold, bewigged thing. To be someone is to be swallowed
by a glass of ice water and to live inside its imperious solitude.
Warhol did his best to pretend the paintings were simply commerce,
more of the same, but they were not the same.
There was death in them. Beneath the nacreous wig he felt it coming.

I went downtown and went down

on the We Buy Gold guy. I have a thing
for debauched hucksters in ape costumes.
Before that I loved the girl who holds the sign

outside Little Caesar's advertising the 2
for 1 pizza deal. Tragic life and long tresses.
She was ghostly, the way she beckoned

to oncoming traffic. Then, the birthday
clown. Nothing worse than jamming
a rubber nose over your nose for a paycheck.

Myself, I've been a fetish-shop cashier, a fudge
worker in Vacationland, played Spidora
in the haunted house, my head sticking out

of the poison gland of a tarantula suit. Wrote
dime-store romances. Was paid a dollar, once,
for a pornographic haiku. Waxed the big

slide, Windexed the jukebox glass, supervised
the shooting gallery. Toilet worker at the sugar
factory, which once involved scooping

a wedding ring out of the loo. The best
was cleaning splooge off the walls in the peep
show gallery and laundering Trixie's thong.

Some of us claw our way to the bottom,
transcend downward. There at the hub
of the drain, we swirl.

My pants are disintegrating. Yes,

my bright pink pants. Bright pink, black tiger stripes.
The pants on which I built my new life.
Pants I'm known for. Foundational. Infamous.

In one day, holes. Old hungers, yawning griefs.
Split incisions. Indecisions. Those pants, sunset
tiger striping the sky. The pink so domestic,

like girl-curtains, a canopy bed. The black
so inkish, so woman writer, so Cleopatra's
mascara. The pink so Sappho's vaginal whorl,

so *Of Woman Born.* The black so Era of Poetess
Suicides. So Tia Maria and Seconals.
It was all so balanced, so joyous, so pitifully bifurcated,

naively bi-curious, so woozy, sleazy, back before
my pants acted all napalmed, all flesh-eating
bacteria, all sloughed-off aesthetic, all glory holed.

Do you remember that spring? The breeze smelled like cake mix

and something in the air of sodomy. Maybe it was the spirea,
which reeks of spermatozoa and Pine-Sol. Don't you miss those days,
the open-mouthed kisses, lips swollen as deer twats in the springtime?
We lived a life of smutty angst and reckless kleptomania at the eye-shadow emporium.
Still pretending to be girls, and hetero, wearing lacy knickers and shit kickers.
We were, relatively speaking, housewives.
Haute cuisine was Bisquick pizza and lychee martinis.
Threw the dirty dishes out the back door into the rhubarb patch.
Plundered the skeletons of burned-down houses for bone china.
Yes, all of our plates died of smoke inhalation.
Remember, somebody kidnapped you and set you up in a whorehouse
in West Virginia. So not cool.
I had to thumb a dangerous ride in order to break you out;
I strode in wearing those tall red boots, a whole red ensemble,
complete with sword masking as parasol.
Yes, gallantry was a fashion statement.
Your recovery required deprogramming and a new hairdo.
Bouffant-cum-beehive with a deep blue rinse and gold highlights.
Remember, we got jobs?
You dabbed mayo on the Jell-O salads at the Amish cafeteria.
I drove the Kowloon noodle truck.
My specialty was delivering post-dated fortune cookies to the less fortunate,
but work kills the dream.
Are you still mainlining amnesia, that downer, or nostalgia, double-downer?
I overdosed long ago and got set up in permanent rehab.
The treatment philosophy is de-lousing and head shaving,
making a present of the present tense.
They clip me to the quick so I don't use my diamond fingernails
to scratch messages into windowpanes.
I just had a flashback to that night we jacked off the conical purple flowers
that hung off the wisteria vine, or did we cluster fuck the floribunda?
The woody stem grew counter clockwise up the ornamental elopement ladder.
Time was all corkscrewed.
We drove an incinerating car the wrong way up a one-way.
Rammed into an orifice designed only as an exit ramp, remember?

Either everything is sexual, or nothing is. Take this flock of poppies,

smoke-green stems brandishing buds the size of green plums, swathed
    in a testicular fur. Even those costumed in the burlesque of red crepe
        petals have cocks under their skirts, powdered with indigo-black pollen,

staining everything they touch. Either the whole world is New Orleans
    at 3 a.m. and a saxophone like a drill bit or it's all clinical sunlight and sad
        elementary school architecture, circa 1962, no broom closets opening into escape

hatches, no cowpokes with globs of sap skewered on hickory sticks. Either
    it's all New York in 1977, the Pan Am building lit up like a honey hive and erecting
        itself out of the fog, and one of us is a junkie and one of us is naked under a gold

skirt safety pinned at the waist and the material melts in the rain, either Kinky
    is playing the Lone Star and earth is the women's john at the tail end of the bar
        and the stall doors have been blow-torched at the hinges and dragged away

by horses, either cunnilingus is an ocean salting every alleyway and lifting
    every veil or the French teacher did not masturbate beneath the desk as he taught
        the subjunctive, and lightning did not cleave the cherry tree and pleasure

its timbers. Either straitjacket, or shock treatment orgasm igniting the dinner theatre,
    the actors cradling and hair-pulling, kissing each other so deep some might call it
        brain surgery, the wigs slipping, chintz curtains aflame, codpieces bursting

into flower, or what's left is a book of wet matches, my dear,
    and it's all been for nothing, for didn't Jesus say you are either
        with me or against me, from out of his blossom of bloodshot dust?

iii. lush

I can't listen to music, especially "Lush Life,"

not as the era of tiger lilies wanes, not as their petals
hang like the tongues of thirsty dogs, and the dusty star

chart of baby's breath, and the brown-eyed Susan's
dark mound wreathed by gold petals like a nipple

bitten black. I long to frolic in the blue snow
of an old television. Long for a bite of a death bed

pomegranate. For the green-haired girl wearing
a pomegranate-hued fedora. So much like my fedora,

but mine is black, and she is young, her body tattooed
with my life story. There is Michigan on the palm

of her hand, New York on her inner thigh. There's Spain
on her coccyx, and the boy who tore into my mouth

on a blanket in a huge bowl of earth outside Madrid,
and around us the throngs shouting *Death to Kissinger.*

There are the almond trees in full flower outside
my bedroom window, and the poisoned strawberries,

so sweet, until later on the train back from Segovia.
I lie on my back in the Retiro, braless, wearing a white

lace blouse. I've cut my own hair and it's short as a nun's.
I'm playing dead, like Lorca did at parties. Hit me

over the head with his sugary femur.
Nostalgia is depression. Who said that?

So let's toast to the present tense.
Vodka and hummingbird nectar, stirred
with a finger bone. Can't even read

the lyrics of that song or look at the sheet
music. Notes buzzing like flies
over an abandoned wedding gown.

Go to cemetery hill for silence
and it's nothing but a landscape
filled with baby grands, keys echoing

sunset, fedora on fire, my nerve endings
lit up like little trees. Hot, whiskey-scented
wind, Strayhorn wind, his woozy breath

on the back of my neck. Such a lush
lush. And the air is lush with ghosts,
standing in line, hats in hands.

"A flower is a lovesome thing"—Strayhorn

There's a fly on the broad, gold cushion of yarrow,
and a fly on the coneflower's swollen center,

and a fly on the pink lily's rusty clitoris,
oh the garden is lush with flies. Takes me back

to that Cuban restaurant in New York
during the garbage strike, the door swathed

in flies, but it didn't stop us, and we fed each other
black beans, their purple juices in the corners

of our mouths, and his hair was fly-colored
but iridescent, in moments, like their wings,

and his smile full of pointed teeth—his love bites
hurt, and opened a red door to a deeper hurt,

and foreshadowed a killing blow. It wouldn't matter
that I'd throw his oily gun into the East River.

Leaving him would kill me, and word of his death
would kill me again, and after the black

beans, that day, we would lean against the juke
box in a dive called Red Rose, and we'd poke

the number of a song I can no longer stomach,
and we'd dance with our hands in each other's

hair, our whiskey-softened lips pressed close,
dying into each other's smashed lush mouths.

Take it a word at a time:
axis
jazz
gray

A phrase:
washed away

An image:
your pointed smile was tinged with the sadness
of a great love for me

A city:
Paris

A hemorrhage:
I'll live a lush life in some small dive
and there I'll be while I rot with the rest
of those whose lives are lonely too

And a shot glass half-filled with music.

Just a dirty shot glass filled with one Strayhorn
phrase. It could work if I'm armed with my black

fedora pushed down hard over my hair, in fact,
let's tuck my hair up under it, let's cock the hat's

angle to hide one eye. Maybe a journey on foot
to wherever they've archived Strayhorn's piano.

Maybe a touch of a black key. Maybe lift the lid
of the piano bench where my archived selves

lie huddled in various states of undress. When
I was a girl, my father's black coffin reminded me

of a piano. A piano without keys. I was young
enough to believe he was playing dead, and my

nightmares were filled with his strange resurrection,
arms loaded with white lilies. The after party

overflowing with music, Nat King Cole's buoyant
version. Sinatra tried to sing it but failed, the tape

archived in a vault somewhere. The song begins
so sweet, then spirals and wanders, diving down

to a repulsive sorrow. My father reclining
on a lush silk pillow, eyes closed, listening.

Let's align ourselves with the night
blooming flowers. Starry-Eyed Midnight
Candy, Angels' Trumpets' distended

orange bells. Operatic face of the Cereus,
spiked as a sea creature. Jasmine's over-sweet
funk. Sun's obsessive light is too much.

Love was always too much. And sex,
its over-stimulations. How about a low-
frequency hum? A trembling

to match my trembling. Insomniac's
garden. Sleepwalker's garden. Tin bell vines
trembling on the rooftops. Bony solo

from the moonflower's white mouth.

I heard it live once, at the Bottom Line, from a wooden chair
in the front row, just below the stage, so Sonny's beat-up shoes

were eye-level, and to watch him blow I had to tip my head back
on its stem and gaze upward, and at one point he opened his eyes

and stared into mine, he directed that brass bell at my face, licked
the reed and blew out a lush stream, I opened my mouth, I didn't

know any better, I was a girl, a girl wearing a cheap white dress
with a lace-up bodice, my fingernails painted like pearls. I loved,

I thought that was the only choice, I splayed myself, I was wet
between the legs, I bled through my dress, onto the wooden chair.

I looked up into the dark for something to bloom by.

It burns my brain, the romance of it. The bitter jazz of it.
Love's axis painfully turning.

Seed of the deathbed pomegranate in the body's mouth.
The siren's song of that seed.

Paris, abandoned. Forsaken. Imagined.
Pink lilies on the café table, petals embellished

with needle marks. I want you, green. Absinthe green.
Nauseous green. Green mint, basil, bile.

I dive into the mush of it, the muck of it. Algae
effervescing. Sparkling foam in a champagne flute.

Dive from the balcony into the lonely rot of it. The lowdown
dive of it. The music of the juke box coin of it, dropping

through the perfumed dark. It burns my brain, romantic
spark of it. Needle turning on the lush black wheel.

iv. free beer

Free beer

I'm the one who can hold a mouthful of salt.
Bring him here, the fool dressed in prison stripes.
I can pray for him, even though his eyes are wild.
I can de-louse the rat.

When I was a kid I invited them all to a puppet show.
There were no puppets; I'd planned no show.
Free beer, I said, and they came.

I've seen a puppet theatre.
It resides in the black cavern behind my eyes.
Thoughts are puppets, dangling from their tangled strings.
Bring him here, the one spinning on gloom's rotisserie.

I'll section an orange for the wretched bastard.
I'll ladle him up a mugful of tears.
Free beer, I'll say, though there is no beer.

I emptied my little wishing well of its emptiness

by filling it with desire. A sorry replacement, really.
Wishes are lovely things. Their synonym being *trinkets*.
My war-torn nightgown, more holes than gown—that
trifling. Desire, sad to say, is sludgy with dead leaves,
fish-rot, twaddle. Its juices are sweet, red-brown,

sassafras root pressed in a vice. It's a greased boar,
typhus-ridden, grunting through the fairgrounds making
the girls scream. Bowling ball, borrowed shoes, score pad,
pencil, sad trophy, burdening my well. Why the poets
lined up behind desire I'll never understand. See how

I run through the Rolodex of metaphors in my head
trying to nail its array of suffocations? That cop I dated.
He was smart enough, kind enough, his favorite book
To Kill a Mockingbird. But he lay on top of me like a giant,
he said *a penny for your thoughts,* that odious phrase. He

wanted to throw his copper in my little well in return
for some inanity trolling through my brain. The thought
for which he paid good money: *Get off me, Sam.*
Thankfully, the so-called Lord divested me of it. Desire.
The load that will turn any horse into a sway-back.

Divested me as a punishment, no doubt, but it's been
a fabulous gift, that excision. When I was a girl they thought
they were killing my spirit by locking me in a closet, but I
loved it in there, in the dark, surrounded by sour tulle.
That's where I found my little wishing well, on the grounds

of a cast-off dollhouse. I raised and lowered the bucket,
a thimble drilled with a tiny hole through which to slip
the rope, a human hair, long and black like my hair is now,
tortured with cheap dye. Back then my hair was soft
and brown and fine as spider web. When someone took

scissors to it as I sat in a folding chair under the cherry
tree, the curls drifted off like mayflies, who spread
their green-gold wings for a day and then die. Die easily.
No trouble at all for a pretty translucency to drift into
transparency, for a ghost to give up the ghost.

We fear the undulant,

the uterine wave, the forlorn sway
of ships leaving harbor

and the rippling *uncut hair of graves.*
We look back at the swells and drifts

of curls. Whose curls? God's.
Sky-wide, luxuriant as the mane

of a buffalo. Father's, spread out
like a girl's bouquet on his deathbed

pillow. Or the indigo whorls
of a deific junkie alone in a shadowy

room, swooning into the arms
of euphoric death, needle

still twanging in the vein
like the fletching of an arrow.

I fear the flickering
of film-school movies on the cave

wall. There I am, bad actress
wearing salt-white gloves,

playing a girl who fears undulant
beauty, undulant love.

I snapped it over my knee like kindling

Then I built a little fire and set a match to it. The flames were purple
at the tip. The purple-pink of moth orchids pinned to a prom dress.

Yes, I snapped desire over my knee and arsoned it. You better believe
there was a soundtrack. Nothing happens without a soundtrack

anymore. Half the time it's Janis, the other half it's some talentless
bum with his thirsty lips wrapped around a mouth harp. Only then,

when desire was just a puny twig fire, did my junkie come back
from the dead. He made a beautiful ghost, fox eyes and deep blue

unruly curls. Arms constellated with needle marks. I thought
of the time he pressed an ice cold can of Coke against my

sunburned ass. Those patent leather boots I wore when I first
got to New York. How he opened my blisters with a razor blade.

I had turned out exactly as he'd said I would. I'd thrown all of my
rings and bracelets into the river. My bloomers and beribboned

corsets, sliced into dust rags. I was scruffy, imperious, off-kilter,
like his Grandma Sally. Limping like Sally, the queen of Riverside

Drive. Hello darlings, she'd call from her seat in front of the easel.
She'd pause mid-brushstroke as she painted one of her strange

little portraits of her cat. Sally had many empty bedrooms.
Many vanity tables covered in rhinestone baubles and dust.

Her deathbed was child-sized, though she was a big woman
with big hair the color of Silver Queen sweet corn. Over the bed

was a small, square window which neatly framed the bridge
that spanned the Hudson. When I bent down to give Sally

a last kiss, I saw that the bridge was made of matchsticks.
Every now and then, one would flare blue and fizzle out.

I wasn't the last person my junkie kissed before he overdosed,
you know. It was Howard, who was prone on his own deathbed,

ruby lesions hickeying his neck. My junkie was loyal to some things,
disloyal to others. His loyalty to the needle was admirable.

Even his ghost, a junkie through and through, heating a spoon
of delirium over the smoldering punk of my ruined ardor.

It wasn't love, but love's template

The face of dawn, secreted beneath a gold mask.
Purple-furred dusk lifted its leg and marked the oily streets.
Skyscrapers scraped the sky until it beaded blood.
Silver light seeped through the needlemarks punched in heaven's sheath.

We walked to Chinatown, always after dark.
Chinatown, not China, but China's wriggling offspring.
So-called lovers fed off of it, chopsticks deep into a whole red snapper.
Chinese-style, the menu read, though not Chinese.

On the Bowery, poets taking notes.
Not so much poets as what passed for poets in those days.
Bums warmed their hands over garbage ignited in burn barrels.
The colors of poets and bums and lovers blazed, a tapestry of a mirage.

Let's not turn it into an epic.
Maybe a fairy tale derived from an epic-derived myth.
Not love, but love's archetype, like the love that goes on in the afterlife.
A state of being devoid of verbs.

He was naked beneath an unbelted green robe.
A party? Hallucination?
Beauties bent over other beauties, gazing into them like coke mirrors.
He wasn't hung, but precise, like a drill bit.

Soup, sex and manholes gave off steam.
Cloud-like, but not clouds.
Foggy shapes painted on a backdrop, inert as a reliquary.
Inert as the idea of God, or God's idea of God.

Being fractured like a bridge or a bone, releasing the marrow of plot.
I was the heroine, fleeing heroin.
I left him frozen in the moment before euphoria strikes the heart.
I visit him sometimes, like one visits a favorite painting in a vast museum.

Laundromat hit by tornado

The bride died. The girl in love
with milkweed pods and god
died laundering her sunbonnet.

The baby born into the hands
of fog and nuns who falsely
claimed she was Chinese died.

She was not Chinese. Three dogs
sparring over a stolen bone died.
Young wife died up to her nipples

in dirty diapers. Widow died
bleaching her dead husband's
shirts for donation. Lonely lady

died skewered on her loneliness;
liar spiked on her lie. Teenage
girl died contemplating her hitchhike

thumb. Hussy died watching
her husband-stealing clothes spiral
in the dryer. I strode shoeless

from the rubble with my wicker
hamper of folded clothes
having survived the twister

of my foolishness, the funnel
cloud of my warped desire.

Jesus, with his cup

The barber, with his mug of warm foam, his badger-hair brush.

My mother and sister and me and the dog, leashed with a measure
of anchor rope, in the hospital parking lot, waving good-bye
to my father from his window on the 7th floor.

Just him and his tumor, rare as the Hope Diamond,
and his flimsy paper cup half-filled with infirmary water.

The lump in my throat, a tea party cup left in the garage all winter,
holding the silver body and wing dust of a dead moth.

The barber, sweeping the day's worth of hair into the basement,
remembering how he'd traveled to Memorial
to lather the face of the dying man and shave him smooth
in his raised hospital bed and sometimes he shaved the faces
of the dead as a favor to the mortician.

Wondering how this particular life was the life that had been chosen for him.

The barber, walking home in the dark
to a late supper of torn bread in a cup of heavy cream.

Even the mayor's wife sipping from a teacup
wreathed in Banded Peacock butterflies wonders, in her loneliness,
why me? Why this cup?

Toad

The grief, when I finally contacted it
decades later, was black, tarry, hot,
like the yarrow-edged side roads
we walked barefoot in the summer.

Sometimes we'd come upon a toad
flattened by a car tire, pressed into
the softened pitch, its arms spread out
a little like Jesus, and it was now

part of the surface of the road, part
of the road's story. Then there was
the live toad I discovered under
the poison leaves of the rhubarb,

hiding there among the ruby stems,
and if you ate those stems raw,
enough of them, you'd shit yourself
for days. It isn't easy to catch a living

thing and hold it until it pees on you
in fear. Its skin was the dull brown
of my father's clothes, my grandfather's
clothes as he stood behind the barber's

chair, clipping sideburns, laying a warm
heap of shaving cream over a bristly chin,
sharpening his straight razor and swiping it
over the foam-covered cheek of my father,

who often shaved twice a day, his beard
was so obstinate, even in the hospital bed.
When I laid a last kiss on his young cheek,
the scraping hurt my lips. Do you ever

wonder, in your heart of hearts,
if God loves you, if the angels love you,
scowling, holding their fiery swords,
radiating green light? If your father

loved you, if he had room to love you,
given his poverty and suffering, or if
a coldness had set in, a cold-bloodedness,
like Keats at the end, wanting a transfusion

of the reader's life blood so he could live
again? Either way, they're all safely
underground, their gentleness or ferocity,
their numb love, and my father's

tar-colored hair, and the fibers of his good
suit softened by wood tannins,
and grandfather's glass eye with its
painted-on mud-colored iris,

maybe all that's left of him in that walnut
box, and Keats and his soft brown clothes,
and the poets before and after him.
But their four-toed emissary sits

in my hand. I feel the quickening pulse
through its underbelly. Hooded eyes,
molasses-tinged, unexpressive,
the seam of its mouth glued shut.

v. a period's period

Oh, I'm a stone

There was no relief from being
human and so I turned to stone
and now there's no relief
from being a stone. I didn't
choose to be a stone.

Who would choose to be a stone?
The stone you pick up on the path
to grandma's house didn't choose
the path of being a stone.
Believe me. I should know.

I'm a stone. Cold, through
and through. Reverend Anne
tossed her rosary beads
from hand to hand and she said
to me you will be cold.

She shivered when she spoke it.
Those beads were like thick cataracts
over muddy eyes. She was a soothsayer.
Her shack smelled of roses
even though there were no roses

in the vicinity. Her saint was Theresa.
Reagan was president. She called him
the man whose press conferences
interrupted soap operas.
Her stories, she called them.

She predicted the child I'd have.
Curly-haired, she said.
His daddy's name will start with a P.
It was a long labor. 48 hours without
relief. They ended up gutting me

to get him out. Silver-blue cord
wrapped around his neck, thick
as mooring rope. She predicted
the eight-point buck would smash
through the windshield

of my fern-green car.
That car was built like a tank
but the motor ended up
in the front seat. Had to use my knife
to put the animal out of its misery.

Warm throat, stiff gray-brown fur,
hot blood, eye hazing over
as the lights went out. Farmer hung him
up in a tree to butcher him. No reason
for that meat to go to waste.

Look at the balls on that fellow.
My white dress blood-drenched.
There by the Great Miami.
Ohio was not good to me.
Curly-haired, Reverend Anne said,

and you'll live by a river that talk-sings,
and things will happen, many things.
Cold, she said. Not a precious stone.
Not even semi-precious.
Just gray and roundish. Little more

than a pebble. And she shivered
and showed me the door.

It's like this

The prayers of non-believers are beautiful like women
desperate to be beautiful are beautiful, but beautiful
in a way that makes God sick a bit like one too many

petit fours. God's also turned off by the prayers
of believers. They're sweaty and overwrought,
not like stalkers but like window peekers, who tend

toward introversion and stuttering, did you know that?
I once cured a window peeker by setting him up with some
speech therapy. God doesn't even go that far. God's thing

is go ahead and set up your own speech therapy.
God doesn't like crowds or cuddling and hates gifts,
which end up stranding the recipient in the Desert

of Endless Gratitude. Begging God doesn't work.
I know begging doesn't work. If it worked, I wouldn't be
so sad. In fact, if you beg, you're sunk. Ask Gerard

Manley Hopkins. Ask Skinny Neckvessel, one of those
fat guys on whom bullies hung a fatal nickname. I tried
doing some research on the surname Neckvessel

and all I got was info on carotid artery disease.
How would you like to be Skinny Neckvessel,
even for a day, a guy who had to enter the door

of his own house sideways, a guy so fat that his only
comfort was three TV dinners and a Mrs. Smith's
Dutch apple pie? God's point of view is that being God

is a lot like being Skinny Neckvessel, that is, really large
and really uncomfortable and filled with bitterness
and filled with pie. Not to mention that Skinny

Neckvessel was shot and killed for cheating at cards
in Milwaukee, Wisconsin. Huge and far from home
and right between the eyes, that's God's point of view.

A poet came to town

At breakfast, he ordered a single ostrich
egg, over easy. I didn't even know you served
ostrich eggs, I said to the waitress. I'd been

coming to this diner my whole life. Oh yeah,
she said, for years. I tried to show the poet
my town. In the little church he thought

the bottles of sacred oils were perfume, and he
dabbed them on his nether regions. The parishioners
smiled in wistful understanding. He kept giving out

his personal phone number to children, "in case
they needed him." He sat in the minister's chair
and the kids, all wearing their matching Sunday

school t-shirts, lined up to get a look at him. I
introduced him to my brother-in-law, a Vietnam
vet who slurs his words and falls on the ground.

Within minutes they were talking about the caesura.
We hustled down a dirt road that parted
the meadow like a comb. This guy, the poet said,

you've got to talk to this guy. I met him
on a previous trip to the hinterlands.
He thinks the answer to everything is potatoes.

The poet laid me down in a patch of violets and ran
his lips over my lips. He licked the corner of my mouth.
There was a grain of sugar, he said. But you like boys,

I said. It's common knowledge. . . . Of course, he said;
I invented the oil that unhinges assholes.
Lyricism, I said. I'm sick of it. No, he said,

quoting Raymond Carver's story "Fat":
"If we had our choice, no. But there is no choice."

I'm full of sadness

As full as a refrigerator on pay day.

My nights are packed with dreams.
Jam-packed as a husband-leaving suitcase.

And did I leave him or dream I left him?

I dream of a red room and wake to a blue room.
In the blue room a man is offering me a $30,000 diamond ring.
His bare ankles poke out of the ends of his pants.
Wear some socks, I say, looking down at my own bare ankles.

Like a small tree strung with too many wind chimes
my false hope drags a screwy music through the neighborhood.

A neighborhood on the decline.
My house teetering on an incline.

I'm bursting with femaleness
like a decapitated saint whose throat spews light the color of straw.

I know I'm female.
In the nursery they put a sad bow in my hair.
I gathered evidence of my girlhood
like a recluse obsessed with berry-picking.

Look at my apron, stained purple.
My empty tin bucket, my purple lips,
purple shits, like the shits of a bear in late spring.

Sadness overruns me.
I'm bee balm, a swarm at my center.
Pollen heavy on the wires of their back legs.
Like gold velvet pantaloons.

I am the Xerox boy
tackling the biggest copy job in the history of copy jobs.
Reproducing original sadness,
toner cartridge running low.

When asked at the ticket office what I am,
I can only answer I am what is speaking this.
Or its homonym. Or its sobbing antonym.

I'm moved by her, that big-nippled girl

with the diminutive vulva. Sometimes when I wipe
after peeing I say the phrase "cow lips" out loud. I
refuse, these days, to romanticize myself. That girl,

her red shoes. If they'd been high heels I would have
ordered her out into the rain, but they were scuffed
flats with a black vinyl abstraction lolling over the top

like the innards of a poppy or an oversized housefly
rubbing its hands together. Her nipples were huge.
It's liberating to say that. Having noticed it, why not

say it? Some will take umbrage. But when I say
"ordered her out into the rain" I mean "extract her
from my imagination." Does that help? My hair

smells like oven cleaner. My tongue is pale; there's
something wrong with my spleen. The girl's nipples,
the size of flying saucers. Her hairstyle from 1964,

the year my father died. Lace stockings and elbow-
length red gloves. Jade earrings shaped like my body.
Stop saying that she could be my daughter. I could

be my daughter, my daughter's daughter. I have
a dead bone in my leg, and eight screws, which have
no structural purpose. They're symbolic; one for each

screw-up. I've brought my hands to my mouth to tamp
down the ruthless tears. Mine are elongated, my tears
not my tits, like El Greco's penitent St. Peter. How can

I say this so you can begin to understand? Her stance,
frontal. Her nipples, emitting their own light, two
asymmetrical baptismal grottos. The slant rhyme

of her stomach, slender but without muscle tone,
punctuated by an off-center belly button, a period's
period. Her vulva, unassailable. No bigger than

a sphinx moth, with just a wisp of hair over the lips,
like the mouth of a little mute puppet. It reminded me
of an envelope of mouse-colored curls that fell out

of the Book of Psalms that time I turned to the Bible
for solace. The faint loops of hair were mine, secreted
away by my mother from my first haircut at the hands

of her father, a barber. My name on the envelope,
the hair like a dead shrew, flattened by time. Mine,
those curls, and not mine, the way the girl wore her

body, hers but not hers, and like Dickinson claimed
and renounced the metrics of the hymn, laying down
dashes like rodent tracks in a pale block of butter.

The girl's sheer black stockings were strewn with them—
Dickinson's dashes—and they sagged a bit, as she'd
refused to hook them to a garter belt. What I feel

for her, let's not call it love. I am love's mother's
fairy godmother, or the premature daughter of love's
daughter's daughter, and anyway, the big-nippled

girl doesn't want my love. She doesn't want anyone's
love. She's post-love; she's post-love's poster child.
Love, for God's sake—look at her bloody little shoes.

Beauty is over

Beauty was four movies ago, the one in which Vaseline was smeared
on the lens to fog the stars beautiful. Now the rabbits' nests are empty,

the dog looking self-satisfied. Feasting on the younger versions of ourselves,
that's what we do. Violets, hunched in their pots on the veranda, rabbit-like

in their stillness. Their pulses still trill, but no one knows. No one need know.
I like my weekends now, unengaged from what is called beauty. No luring.

Perfuming. Pondering my purple eyelids. Their fluttering. I let my hair go
rank, my body smell of body. The UPS man eyes the hair under my arms

as I sign for his heavy box of ashes. He shivers, thanks God his little wife
at home waxes herself smooth, doesn't lumber or reek like a bear or limp

to the door like some peg-leg, some Igor. An unbeautiful woman is her own
antidote. Her own black granite basilica. Go ahead. Walk in, though you must

enter via her unshaved vulva, oh the vines, the vines, the brambles that break
all axe heads and mastheads! If she is ashamed, she is an implosion of sacred

spaces. If unashamed, she's a foul explosion of barbells and stars, crucifixes
crosshatching the air black. She's the Bigger Bang, creation's recreation,

spewing out purple-tongued trees and animals who glorify in their two-
headedness. Oh little lamb in my red brick hometown museum, one head

gazing west, the other, east, the precious freak who lives at the heart of me
still. All of the new world leaders shall be those born with too many, too much,

the three-eyed, the four-legged, like twelve-fingered Lucille, with her bad
kidneys, bad teeth and bad breasts, her bad hair, her two-headed poetry, my

titanium leg and screws, my stretch marks and wide caesarian scar, my overt
and covert badness, my bad shoes and bare ankles, my badbadbadbad poetry.

Is there still a Betty in this new life?

Still a mortuary of roses, a canvas of starlings?
Still silken teabags filled with dried wasps?

My mind's a tri-level house, a different brand of headache in every room.
I carried the garbage to the curb, placing my bare feet gingerly on black ice.

Is grief still as grand as the blue whale-sized embalming table?
Is love that ballroom hung with Monet's water lilies where I succumbed to morning sickness?
Is there space in the small-town funeral parlor for a blue uterus the size of a boxcar?

I loved Billy, but only for his wooden leg.
I loved the mortician's children for their access to the mortuary.
I loved the paper trees, but only for the moment sunset's hilarity set them on fire.

Is there still a Jesus language on the lips of talking birds?
Is there a Betty, speaking Italian if the language of the dead is Italian?

What holy trinity is dreaming the dreams I'm dreaming?
Is there a beautiful nostalgia like a breeze lifting the purple funeral-parlor curtains?

Is there a Betty gathering the flotsam of the dynamited Buddhas of Afghanistan?

A Betty, reading the bones of my skull with her small hands?

Oh four-legged girl, it's either you or the ossuary

For, having met you on the road to Ramptown

For, having taken notice of your four striped socks, green and plum they were,
or more truthfully, green and lilac, or emerald and heliotrope, and your
four black button-up boots, eleven buttons, not quite twelve, if there were
twelve I would already be in the churchyard

For, having witnessed you on the road to Ramptown, the extra legs hanging
useless between the thighs of the other two, useless as a mechanical
nightingale, I sang under my breath, useless as the fringe from your
Transylvanian kimono

For, having beheld your eyes, dull roadside pennies, dull overused thimbles,
and your skin, gray as the pattern factory on the gravel-laced riverbank
and its two-legged trouser patterns, and the four spit curls snaked against
your forehead, your forehead like a mausoleum-dome, upended sugar bowl

For, having feasted on your four-holed knickers and your skirt the color of crocus
stamens and the silhouette of the witch-boot on your sideways-twisted foot
and your four knees, naked as onion bulbs, and the black, hammered-velvet
bow tying back the circus whips of your hair

For, having fathomed you from my hiding place behind the catalpa tree infested
with sphinx worms as you uncocooned yourself from the layers and leathers
they'd veiled you in, your body oddly silver in the noonday light as you limped
through the encampment of the long-gone runaways

For, having imagined your body one way I found it to be another way, it was yielding,
but only as the Destroying Angel mushroom yields, its softness allied
with its poison, and your legs were not petals or tendrils as I'd believed,
but brazen, the deviant tentacles beneath the underskirt of a secret queen

For, having brooded on you in the leek fields of Ramptown
I'm besotted, harrowed.
It's you or the polyandrium.
You or the bone house.

Acknowledgments

Academy of American Poets "Poem-A-Day": "Toad"

Ampersand: "Oh, I'm a stone" and "I'm full of sadness"

Blackbird: "I went downtown and went down," "Either everything is sexual, or nothing is. Take this flock of poppies," "We fear the undulant," "As a child I ate and mourned," "It's like this," "A poet came to town," and "Is there still a Betty in this new life?"

Black Warrior Review: "Oh four-legged girl, it's either you or the ossuary"

Brevity: "I can't stop thinking of that New York skirt, turquoise sequins glued onto sea colored cotton"

Columbia Poetry Review: "It seems, back then, there was a mythic teapot" and "Long, long ago I used to smoke in bed"

Court Green: "An occasion is a rare occasion"

Crab River Review: "It wasn't love, but love's template" and "Beauty is over"

Ecotone: "People, the ghosts down in North-of-the-South aren't see-through" and "I'm moved by her, that big-nippled girl"

The Georgia Review: "Spirea's covered in those clotted blooms"

Green Mountains Review: "Laundromat hit by tornado" and "Jesus, with his cup"

Hanging Loose: "I once fought the idea of the body as artifact," and "It wasn't a dream, I knew William Burroughs"

Mid-American Review: "I emptied my little wishing well of its emptiness"

The Missouri Review: "I can't listen to music, especially 'Lush Life,'" "White violet, not so much an image," "I snapped it over my knee like kindling," and "Free beer"

Moose and Pussy: "Do you remember that spring? The breeze smelled like cake mix"

New Orleans Review: "Jump rope song"

The Smoking Poet: "My pants are disintegrating. Yes,"

Tar River Poetry: "The potato sack filled with toys was beautiful"

Valparaiso Poetry Review: "Maybe the fishmonger, who hands over the dead"

Wag's Revue: "Hub"

Witness: "Warhol's *Shadows*"

"Either everything is sexual, or nothing is. Take this flock of poppies," appeared in *Pushcart Prize XXXVII: Best of the Small Presses,* Pushcart Press, 2012.

"Free beer" appeared in *The Best American Poetry 2014,* David Lehman, Terrance Hayes, editors, Scribner, 2014.

My gratitude to Hedgebrook, for space, community, and fresh figs, and to Kalamazoo College, for allowing me to camp on the margins and teach. Profound appreciation to Laura Kasischke, Patrick Donnelly, Tony Hoagland, and Jeff Shotts, for their deep and tangible encouragement, and to Conrad Hilberry, who found me, sent me books, helped me go to college, and taught me about humility. Thank you to Gail Wronsky, for hitchhiking and archetypal girl love, Mikel Lindzy, for uncategorizable tenderness, even in death, and Kevin Goldfarb, for schooling me in desire and its price. Abiding love to my mother, who gave me strength and wildness, my father, muse of gentleness and suffering, my sister, who built a house with me under the mock orange tree, my nieces, survivors, all, and Gail Griffin, for enduring friendship, hilarity, and handing me the broom. Finally, my love to Dylan: conundrum, enigma, son.

DIANE SEUSS is the author of six poetry collections, including *Modern Poetry*; *frank: sonnets*, winner of the Pulitzer Prize, the National Book Critics Circle Award, the Los Angeles Times Book Prize, and the PEN/ Voelcker Award; *Still Life with Two Dead Peacocks and a Girl*, a finalist for the National Book Critics Circle Award and the Los Angeles Times Book Prize; and *Four-Legged Girl*, a finalist for the Pulitzer Prize. In 2020, she received a Guggenheim Fellowship, and in 2021, she received the John Updike Award from the American Academy of Arts and Letters. She lives in rural Michigan.

The text of *Four-Legged Girl* is set in Adobe Garamond Pro. Book design by Rachel Holscher. Composition by Bookmobile Design & Digital Publisher Services, Minneapolis, Minnesota. Manufactured by Versa Press on acid-free, 30 percent postconsumer wastepaper.